Titles in Series S892

Little Tommy Tucker and other nursery rhymes

Little Jack Horner and other nursery rhymes

Little Bo Peep and other nursery rhymes

Little Miss Muffet and other nursery rhymes

British Library Cataloguing in Publication Data
Little Tommy Tucker and other nursery rhymes.
  I. Bracken, Carolyn
  398'.8
  ISBN 0-7214-9590-7

First edition

Published by Ladybird Books Ltd Loughborough Leicestershire UK
Ladybird Books Inc Auburn Maine 04210 USA

Printed in England

Little Tommy Tucker

and other nursery rhymes

Illustrated by Carolyn Bracken

Ladybird Books

Jack and Jill went up the hill,
To fetch a pail of water;
Jack fell down, and broke his crown,
And Jill came tumbling after.

Little Tommy Tucker
Sings for his supper;
What shall we give him?
White bread and butter.

How shall he cut it
Without a knife?
How will he be married
Without a wife?

Ride a cock-horse to Banbury Cross,
To see a fine lady upon a white horse;
With rings on her fingers and bells on her toes,
She shall have music wherever she goes.

Old King Cole was a merry old soul,
And a merry old soul was he;
He called for his pipe,
And he called for his bowl,
And he called for his fiddlers three.

Dance to your daddy,
My little laddie,
Dance to your daddy, my little lamb!
You shall have a fishy
In a little dishy,
You shall have a fishy,
When the boat comes in.

Dance to your daddy,
My little laddie,
Dance to your daddy, my little lamb!
You shall have an apple,
You shall have a plum,
You shall have a rattle-basket,
When your dad comes home.

Here we go round
　　　the mulberry bush,
The mulberry bush,
　　　the mulberry bush.
Here we go round
　　　the mulberry bush,
On a cold and
　　　frosty morning!

This is the way we
　　　wash our clothes,
Wash our clothes,
　　　wash our clothes.
This is the way we
　　　wash our clothes,
On a cold and
　　　frosty morning!

Girls and boys, come out to play,
The moon is shining bright as day;
Leave your supper, and leave your sleep,
And come with your playfellows into the street.
Come with a whoop and come with a call,
Come with a good will or not at all.
Come let us dance on the open green,
And she who holds longest shall be our queen.

Georgie Porgie, pudding and pie,
Kissed the girls and made them cry;
When the boys came out to play,
Georgie Porgie ran away.

Elsie Marley is grown so fine,
She won't get up to feed the swine,
But lies in bed till eight or nine;
Lazy Elsie Marley.

This little piggy
went to market.

This little piggy
stayed home.

This little piggy
had roast beef.

This little piggy
had none.

And this little piggy said, "Wee, wee, wee,"
All the way home.

To market, to market, to buy a fat pig,
Home again, home again, jiggety jig.
To market, to market, to buy a fat hog,
Home again, home again, jiggety jog.

One, two, three, four, five,
Once I caught a fish alive.
Why did you let it go?
Because it bit my finger so.

Six, seven, eight, nine, ten,
Shall we go to fish again?
Not today, some other time,
For I have broken my fishing line.

Ding, dong, bell, pussy's in the well.
Who put her in? Little Johnny Green.
Who pulled her out? Little Tommy Stout.

What a naughty boy was that,
To try to drown poor pussy cat,
Who never did him any harm,
And killed the mice
        in his father's barn.

Pussy cat, pussy cat, where have you been?
I've been to London to look at the queen.
Pussy cat, pussy cat, what did you there?
I frightened a little mouse under her chair.

If I'd as much money
  as I could spend,
I never would cry,
  "Old chairs to mend,
Old chairs to mend,
  old chairs to mend."
I never would cry,
  "Old chairs to mend."

If I'd as much money
  as I could tell,
I never would cry,
  "Old clothes to sell,
Old clothes to sell,
  old clothes to sell."
I never would cry,
  "Old clothes to sell."

Hark, hark, the dogs do bark,
The beggars are coming to town;
Some in rags and some in jags,
And some in velvet gowns.

Polly, put the kettle on,
Polly, put the kettle on,
Polly, put the kettle on,
We'll all have tea.

Sukey, take it off again,
Sukey, take it off again,
Sukey, take it off again,
They've all gone away.

Pease porridge hot, pease porridge cold,
Pease porridge in the pot, nine days old.

Some like it hot,
Some like it cold,

Some like it in the pot,
Nine days old.

Rub-a-dub-dub, three men in a tub,
And who do you think they be?
The butcher, the baker, the candlestick-maker;
Turn 'em out, knaves all three.

Here am I,
Little Jumping Joan;
When nobody's with me,
I'm all alone.

Jack, be nimble,
Jack, be quick,
Jack, jump over the candlestick.

There was an old woman tossed up in a basket,
Seventeen times as high as the moon;
And where she was going, I couldn't but ask it,
For under her arm she carried a broom.

Old woman, old woman, old woman, said I,
Where are you going to up so high?
To sweep the cobwebs from the sky!
May I go with you? Aye, by and by.

Diddle diddle dumpling, my son John
Went to bed with his trousers on;
One shoe off, and one shoe on,
Diddle diddle dumpling, my son John.